TIMES PAST
YORKSHIRE

SUSAN NOWAK

*This book is part of the Times Past series, produced using
photographs from the archives of the Hulton Picture Library
including many from the famous Picture Post magazine.*

Top: BRIDLINGTON BEACH, 1912;
BOTTOM, LEFT TO RIGHT: TOP WITHINS, THE SETTING FOR WUTHERING HEIGHTS, 1955;
YORK MINSTER FROM STONEGATE, c1930; ROBIN HOOD'S BAY, 1910.

MYRIAD
LONDON

LEEDS

The industrial revolution fuelled the expansion of Leeds, turning it into one of the great Victorian cities of England. Engineering, textiles, chemicals, pottery and coal all contributed to its success and led to the construction of some of the city's prestigious civic buildings.

ABOVE: **THE CORN EXCHANGE, 1874.** The Corn Exchange was completed in 1864 and designed by the architect Cuthbert Broderick who was also responsible for Leeds Town Hall. The vast oval hall let in direct sunlight through the roof windows, allowing those valuing the corn samples to make a more accurate assessment.

ABOVE: **POST OFFICE, 1921.** The Post Office was built in 1896 on the north side of City Square by architect Sir Henry Tanner. The building and its position at the centre of the city reflected Victorian Leeds' need for good communications and a prosperous business and commercial community.

ABOVE: **BOAR LANE, 1921.** At the beginning of the 19th century Boar Lane was still a residential road with fine merchants' houses but by the 1860s it was also a major shopping street, with many of the buildings reflecting the popular French influence of the time.

ABOVE: **CITY SQUARE AND THE BLACK PRINCE STATUE, 1921.** The Black Prince statue was the brainchild of the City's Lord Mayor, Thomas Walter Harding, as a celebration of Leeds' new city status in 1893. It was unveiled in 1903 in the new civic space of City Square and surrounded by fine Victorian buildings including the General Post Office and Mill Hill Unitarian Chapel.

ABOVE: **PAPER SELLER, 1931.** Street vendors like this boy, with the Leeds Mercury, were common on every street corner up until the Second World War.

LEFT: **NEW BRIGGATE, 1921.** Briggate has been a major shopping centre in Leeds since mediaeval times, first as a market and then with large stores and elegant indoor arcades. New Briggate was opened in 1868, with some of the development being in the very popular mock Tudor-style.

ABOVE: **LAUNDRY BLOCKADE, 1937.** Workers' housing was largely unregulated and thrown up as quickly as possible at incredibly high densities. A characteristic of the Leeds area was that houses were built in terraces, back-to-back with the next row, with the front door opening directly onto the street. The street was the only place for women to hang out the washing.

ABOVE: **SCRAP METAL, 1935.** Recycling is nothing new and there was considerable money to be made out of scrap metal before the war. Customers searching through the yard for cheap spares cannot have failed to notice the many posters for local cinemas and sporting fixtures surrounding the entrance.

RIGHT: **STREET SWEEPING, 1913.** In December 1913, 3,000 Leeds corporation workers went on strike in support of higher pay. Gasworkers stopped work causing black-outs all over Leeds and extra police were drafted in. There were bomb attacks on the gasworks and the army barracks. In the streets rubbish lay uncollected, so shopkeepers decided to take things into their own hands.

ABOVE: **QUARRY HILL, 1939.** By the late 1930s there was a real desire to pull down the Victorian slums. The response of planners and architects to the challenge of rehousing so many people was to build enormous high-rise developments such as Quarry Hill. It had a shopping centre, nursery school and a built-in refuse disposal system. However, the flats soon became beset with social and structural problems and were demolished in 1978.

ABOVE: **IN THE MIRROR, 1939.** Working on the buses, trams or trains was a job to be proud of and it was important to be correctly turned out. Clean cap, polished badge, neat hair, and a close shave were all essentials for a conductor or driver as the mirror at Swinegate Bus Depot attests.

LEFT: **VICTORIA ARCADE, 1931.** Covered shopping arcades are a special feature of Leeds. The Victoria Arcade was designed by Thomas Ambler, who was also responsible for the Leeds Permanent Building Society building and the Trevelyan Hotel. The Victoria Arcade has now been redeveloped and incorporated into the new Schofields' Shopping Centre.

Cricket

The words cricket and Yorkshire are almost synonymous. Len Hutton, Brian Close, Freddie Trueman, Ray Illingworth and Geoffrey Boycott are just some of the many first-class cricketers to have played for the County and for England.

Above: **YORKSHIRE TEST, 1928.** The famous Yorkshire cricket ground at Headingley is said to attract some of the most knowledgeable cricket fans in the country. This Test match against Australia in 1926 was drawn but England went on to win the series 1-0 and regain the Ashes after three consecutive defeats.

Right: **THE MAJOR AND THE BOYS, 1926.** Major AW Lupton, a 43-year-old Bradford wine and spirits merchant, was appointed as captain of Yorkshire in 1924 after lapses of protocol and discipline in the previous season. Good social standing and a firm approach to discipline were the requisites for the job. The "boys" pictured with the Major are George Hirst and Wilfred Rhodes. Hirst and Rhodes were two of the most outstanding cricketers ever to play for Yorkshire, setting unbeaten records for both runs and wickets.

LEFT HUTTON AND YARDLEY, 1946. Len Hutton was one of England and Yorkshire's finest batsmen and the first professional captain of England. He was arguably the most successful, never losing a Test series, and both winning (for the first time in 20 years) and defending the Ashes against Australia. Norman Yardley also held both captaincies in the late 1940s. He was also an outstanding hockey and squash player.

BELOW: TRUEMAN THE TERROR, 1953. Freddie Trueman was described as the greatest threat ever faced by Australia in the 1950s. A powerful fast bowler, he was also often outspoken, which on occasion got him into trouble with England's management. Today he brings his own blunt style to the world of cricket commentary.

ABOVE: RECORD-BREAKERS, 1932. Herbert Sutcliffe and Percy Holmes, one of the great partnerships of the 1920s and 1930s, pictured after breaking the record for first wicket stands when they made 555 runs for Yorkshire against Essex.

BELOW: CITY CRICKET, 1953. Cricket is said to run through the blood of every Yorkshireman. The chance to play a game, wherever it is possible, is amply demonstrated here by these boys on this wasteland site just outside the centre of Leeds.

SHEFFIELD

Like Rome, Sheffield developed on seven hills, carved by six rivers, which provided the power for wheels to grind the steel for which the city is famous.

ABOVE: **CRIMEA MONUMENT, 1870.** The Crimea monument was erected at Moorhead in 1863 by public subscription, as a memorial to the citizens of the town who fell in the Crimean War. In 1957 it was removed for a road-widening scheme and was subsequently re-erected in parts with the figure of Victory and the stone plinth going to the Botanical Gardens and the marble column to a playground in Upperthorpe. Its future is once again under discussion and it may soon return to the city centre.

ABOVE: **SHEFFIELD SLUMS, 1936.** These dwellings in the Button Lane district of the city were photographed shortly before demolition.

RIGHT: **PEACE PARADE, 1919.** After the First World War ended King George V (1865-1936) undertook a royal tour to celebrate the return of peace. Sheffield had good reason to celebrate. The Sheffield Battalion was set up one month after the start of the Great War and 1,000 men were recruited in just two days. Half were killed at the Battle of Serre in 1916 and subsequent battles also took a heavy toll.

Above: **MARKET PLACE, SHEFFIELD** *c*1890. At this time, the Market Place in Sheffield consisted of an irregular sprawl of shops and stalls, surrounded by High Street, Swine Market, Bullstake (later renamed Haymarket) and King Street (also known as Pudding Lane).

Above: **HOLIDAYS AT HOME, 1943.** A family return home after a day out. During the war, holidays away from home were a rarity. However, most workers were entitled to paid leave and the day trip became a popular pastime, either by train or charabanc. From Sheffield day trips could be taken to the coastal resorts or to the Peak District just a few miles west of the city centre.

Left: **WINCOBANK, 1938.** This photograph of Wincobank and the surrounding countryside was taken from the top of the Sheffield Gas Company's giant gasholder during an inaugural visit by the Duke of Kent. Wincobank is the site of an iron-age hill fort and is possibly Sheffield's earliest settlement. When the gasholder was opened it was the largest spiral-guided gasholder in the world; fully inflated it reached a height of 234ft (71m).

SHEFFIELD AND STEEL-MAKING

Sheffield has been famous for making steel since the middle ages – especially the manufacture of cutlery. In 1913, Harry Brearley, an employee of the Sheffield company Thomas Frith and Sons, produced the first stainless steel – a major breakthrough in the history of metal-making.

ABOVE: **STEEL MILL, 1955.** During the Second World War, Sheffield steel plants manufactured large amounts of armaments and the city became a prime target for German bombing raids. But within a few years, the industry was back on its feet. In the 1950s, around 130 Sheffield firms employing 41,000 workers produced over three-quarters of the UK's steel.

BELOW: **SMELTING STEEL, 1949.** George Goodwin, a steel potter, was photographed by *Picture Post* magazine for an article on the Sheffield steel industry. His job is to produce the clay for the crucibles in which steel is smelted.

LEFT: **CITY OF STEEL, 1940.** The tall smoking chimney stacks of a steel-rolling mill dominate the skyline of the Don Valley to the north-east of the city centre.

ABOVE: **GRINDING FORKS, 1955.** An employee of a Sheffield factory finishes the prongs of a fork on a thin wheel. It was widely believed that the superior quality of local grindstones was a major reason why Sheffield was the world leader in the production of cutlery.

BELOW: **KNIFE-MAKING, 1932.** Sharpening knives on a grindstone at Sphere Commission. Cutlery production involves a number of small stages and is very labour intensive. During the Second World War, Sheffield companies produced millions of knives for the armed forces.

LEFT: **HAMMERING STEEL, 1932.** Once the blades have been forged, shaped and sharpened the handles are fitted. The history of the city records over 100 specialised knife manufacturers including famous names such as Wolstenholm, Mappin, Rodgers and Butcher.

Yorkshire mining

Coal from the Yorkshire coalfields has long been one of Britain's most important sources of power. At its height, one million workers were employed in the pits in Yorkshire and Lancashire alone. Today there are just a couple of thousand miners left in the county.

ABOVE: **ASKERN COLLIERY, 1940.** During the 18th and 19th centuries Askern, near Doncaster, was known for the healing properties of the local water and a spa was established. But in the 1900s a rich seam of coal was discovered and a mine was built. Mining and health were at odds and at the start of the Second World War the spa closed. In 1991 the mine was shut and the slag heaps are now being cleaned and replanted as a woodland and wildlife area.

BELOW: **WENTWORTH WOODHOUSE, 1945.** Wentworth Woodhouse dates from the 18th century and was built for the wealthy Wentworth family. Its gardens, which were landscaped by Humphrey Repton (1752-1818), were almost destroyed during the Second World War by open-cast mining. After the war the house became a teacher-training college but is now a private home.

Above: **BARNSLEY COLLIERY**, *c*1945. If there was one town that was synonymous with coalmining it was Barnsley. The great pit-heads and spoil heaps of the collieries surrounding the town cast an environmental blight over the whole area. Mining was an industry that provided a living and in many cases an early death for more than a century. Today those bleak landscapes have been transformed and replanted and the town is marketing itself as a tourist destination.

Left: **PIT BOY JOCKEYS**, 1925. Even as late as the 1920s boys as young as 14 could be employed to work down the mines. Often they were put in charge of the pit ponies that pulled the coal along the tunnels to the pit shaft. Here, in a lighter moment, the boys are on their way to take part in a pit pony race meeting at Thorp, near Wakefield.

Left: **LOADING COAL**, 1942. In July 1942 *Picture Post* went to West Yorkshire to report on the mining of outcrop coal. The wartime Ministry of Fuel and Power was engaged on a drive to increase coal production to meet the demand for fuel to power the munitions factories which were working round the clock. Huge excavators were used to work coal seams near the surface; this allowed men with no previous experience of mining to achieve productivity rates far in excess of deep-cast mines.

Right: **MECHANICAL MINING**, 1942. A tractor driver works an open seam in the West Riding.

HALIFAX AND HUDDERSFIELD

On the edge of the Pennines, the towns of Huddersfield and Halifax both owe much of their heritage to the textile industry, which has left a fine legacy of Victorian buildings and spin-offs into other associated manufacturing. In recent years, Huddersfield has reinvented itself as a creative and media centre.

ABOVE: **INDUSTRIAL SKYLINE, 1958.** By the 1950s the factories of Halifax were producing textiles, textile machinery, household goods and building materials. The inevitable consequence from the smoking chimneys was considerable pollution. While the Clean Air Act was passed by Parliament in 1956 it was some years before it took effect.

BELOW: **SURVEYING THE SCENE, 1955.** An elderly resident of Halifax looks out over the town.

RIGHT: **ROYAL FOLLOWERS, 1949.** Huge, happy crowds followed Princess Elizabeth and Prince Philip on their tour of Yorkshire in 1949 as witnessed at Huddersfield football stadium. The local football team, Huddersfield Town, were the first to win the football league three years in a row. The stadium has now been replaced with the futuristic Alfred McAlpine stadium, which is home to both the football and rugby league teams. Rugby league was born at the George Hotel in Huddersfield.

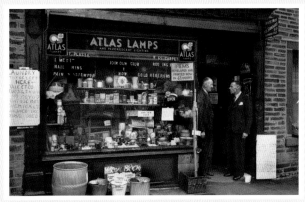

ABOVE: **SHOP SALESMAN, 1953.** Ironmongers' shops were a feature of every small shopping parade in the 1950s. The shops sold a wide range of products including carpets, electrical fittings, crockery, cleaning and building materials. This shop in Halifax also processed films. The travelling salesman was an important figure, introducing shop-owners to new products about which it would have been difficult to discover information in any other way.

RIGHT: **MOTORISED PAPER BOY, 1962.** The weekly Huddersfield District Chronicle was founded in 1927 as the Dearne Valley Advertiser, the "weekly voice of the South-Eastern districts of Huddersfield". Here the circulation manager is out checking whether the paper is reaching subscribers.

ABOVE: **STUD PRODUCTION, 1958**. The man who created "cat's-eyes", which were described in the House of Commons as "the most brilliant invention ever produced in the interests of road safety", was Halifax-born Percy Shaw. Here he is seen, supervising the production of the component parts at his factory in Boothtown, Halifax.

LEFT: **MAKING FIREWORKS, 1930.** Huddersfield has a long association with firework-making, which was considered to be women's work. Standard Fireworks set up in the town in 1920. Now part of the Black Cat Group, Britain's largest firework producer, they continue to manufacture fireworks in the town.

BRADFORD

*Bradford's growth was built on the back of the woollen and worsted
industry for which it became the leading centre in the world. Thousands
of people flocked to Bradford to find work in the town's textile factories.
A legacy of wonderful Victorian mills and civic buildings remains.*

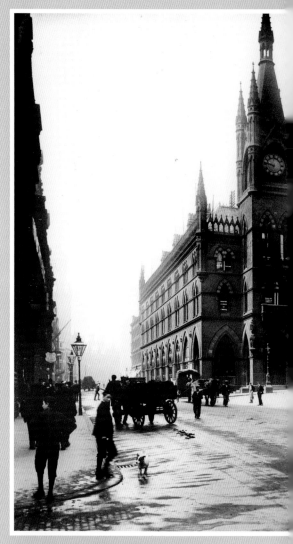

ABOVE: **BRADFORD TOWN HALL, 1921.** As Bradford grew it became clear that a
purpose-built civic building was needed. A competition to design a town hall was
launched in 1869. The winning submission was that of local architects Lockwood
and Mawson. The town hall took three years to build at a cost of £100,000. Its
most notable feature is the magnificent Italianate-style clock tower that soars
220ft (67m) above the skyline.

RIGHT: **THE WOOL EXCHANGE, 1921.** The Wool Exchange is a tribute to Bradford's
industrial past when traders from all over the world haggled for the best
merchandise inside its cavernous hall. It too was designed by Lockwood and
Mawson in ornate Venetian-style after winning a competition. It has recently
been refurbished and converted into a shopping centre.

RIGHT: **FORSTER
SQUARE,** *c*1900.
Forster Square lies
at the heart of the
old town and was
the transport hub of
Bradford with its
own railway station
and a plethora of
trolleybus routes.
The square was
named after William
Forster, a Bradford
MP and the minister
responsible for
introducing the 1870
Education Act

which introduced compulsory state education for all Britain's elementary pupils.

RIGHT: **LEEDS ROAD, 1921.** While sheep being driven along Leeds Road in Bradford
was not a common sight in 1921, the cart on the left of the picture carrying huge
sacks of wool was. The company of SW Whaley & Son started life in 1863 as a
manufacturer of silk and jute. It is still in business specialising in producing
flame-proof fabrics, fashion fabrics, theatre curtains and bags for the coal and
textile industries.

Left: **BRADFORD STREET, 1940.** A solitary car makes its way down a Bradford street, past terraces of workers' houses and with the pollution from the mill chimneys only too evident. Dimly through the smoke the moors can be seen beyond.

Above: **LISTER'S MILLS, 1921.** When Lister's Mills or Manningham Mill opened in the 1870s it was the most imposing textile factory anywhere in the north of England. Built in the popular Italianate-style with an impressive 250ft (76m) chimney it replaced a mill which was destroyed by fire. It occupies 27 acres and at one time employed 11,000 people.

Fishing

For hundreds of years there have been fishing fleets in every port up and down the Yorkshire coast from Hull to Whitby. The photographs here give an insight into a way of life steeped in centuries-old tradition.

BELOW: **FISHERFOLK, c1880.** Frank Meadows Sutcliffe (1853-1941) chronicled the lives of the fishing communities of Whitby and Robin Hood's Bay. This photograph of fisherfolk with their lobster pots is one of his most famous images.

RIGHT: **HERRING HARVEST, 1907.** Women gut the herring and pack the fish into wooden barrels as the catch is unloaded on the quayside at Scarborough. During the herring season an army of workers would follow the fleets from one fishing town to another to help with fish processing. Foreign herring fishing boats flocked to Scarborough and other coastal towns during the herring season until the 1970s. As with cod, over-fishing has sounded the death knell of the industry. The Scarborough Centre for Coastal Studies, part of Hull university, is carrying out research into how fish populations can be sustained.

RIGHT: **OLD HARBOUR, HULL, 1921.** Warehouses surround the harbour at Hull which was first developed in the 15th century by a merchant family called the De La Poles. Sir William De La Pole became Hull's first mayor in 1331. Today the area has been transformed with waterside housing and shopping developments.

Above: **Fishergirls, 1951.** Onshore fish processing became increasingly important to the economy of Hull in post-war Britain. The work was hard, smelly and often freezing cold. Wages for those working in the industry in the 1950s were relatively good, despite the poor living conditions shown in this photograph by *Picture Post* photographer Bert Hardy.

Left: **Whitby Dockside, 1937.** Yorkshire ports – Hull, Scarborough, Filey and Whitby – dominated the British fishing industry for much of the 20th century.

Above: **Cod Catch, 1934.** Freshly caught cod in the fish market at Hull. For centuries cod was the staple catch of Hull's deep sea fishing industry, which is not surprising given that Britons eat up to one third of the world's cod catch every year. But perhaps not for much longer: cod has been over-fished and rigorously enforced quotas are in place throughout Europe.

YORK

The history of York spans two millennia with a legacy that includes the Romans and the Vikings. In recent times, railways and manufacturing have brought prosperity; today the city is one of Britain's leading tourist destinations.

RIGHT: **THE SHAMBLES, 1890.** The mediaeval Shambles, with its timber-clad houses, is one of York's most visited streets. By the mid-50s (below) the medieval shops and houses had been beautifully restored. The word "shambles" derives from *shamel* meaning bench or stall; from the 15th to the 19th centuries the street was full of butchers' stalls. At the narrowest point of the Shambles it is possible for two people to touch hands across the street.

BOTTOM: **LENDAL BRIDGE AND LENDAL TOWER, *c*1910.** Rowers on the River Ouse pass underneath Lendal Bridge. Built in 1863 it replaced a ferry service that had taken passengers across the river Ouse since the Middle Ages.

ABOVE: **NEWGATE, 1956.** York Minster looms large against the backdrop of the mediaeval buildings surrounding the market square. Over the centuries, York has had many markets, but from the Victorian period there was just one, a daily one sited in Parliament Street and St Saviour's Square. In 1955 the market moved to Newgate, which is sited between Parliament Street and the Shambles.

LEFT: **SIR THOMAS HERBERT'S HOUSE, PAVEMENT,** *c*1949. Sir Thomas Herbert was born in this house near the Shambles in 1606. He was a true 17th-century cavalier, traveller and adventurer, receiving personal gifts from Charles I for services rendered. The house dates from the mid 16th century and still boasts one of the finest oak mantelpieces in the country as well as wall paintings. Extensive renovations were carried out to the house during the 1920s.

RIGHT: **ROYALS IN YORK, 1949.** Crowds line Stonegate as Princess Elizabeth (now Queen Elizabeth) steps out with the Mayor and the Duke of Edinburgh on the third day of the royal tour of the West Riding and Yorkshire. The name Stonegate is derived from the road's use as the route along which the stones for York Minster were carted from the river.

Harrogate

Harrogate nestles on the southern edge of the Yorkshire Dales. By the end of the 19th century Harrogate was one of England's leading spas, and possibly its most aristocratic. It attracted many visitors to stay for up to three weeks in its magnificent hotels, sampling the waters and taking a range of hydrotherapeutic treatments.

Top: **THE STRAY AND THE PROSPECT HOTEL, 1880.** Elegant riders and carriages on the Stray, with the Prospect Hotel in the background. The Stray Act of 1770 secured free public access to 200 acres of open space named the Stray for the people of Harrogate. The act was prompted by fears that the land, which contained many of the mineral springs, would be enclosed, effectively privatising the waters and affecting the livelihood of local people. The Prospect Hotel, now the Yorkshire Hotel, is typical of the many large hotels built for spa visitors.

ABOVE: **THE ROYAL BATHS, 1919.** The Royal Baths were opened by HRH the Duke of Cambridge in 1897. The interior was in Moorish style, with huge Islamic arches and beautiful glazed brickwork walls. A wide range of facilities was available including a medicinal waters' dispensary, hydrotherapy departments, mud baths and steam rooms, as well as a full complement of consulting doctors. The Turkish Baths remain in daily operation.

ABOVE: **THE VALLEY GARDENS, 1921.** Fashionable women promenade through the elegant gardens which have helped to cement Harrogate's claim to be "England's Floral District". Acres of beautifully planted beds lead out of town from the Pump Room to pines, woods and the Dales beyond. Boating, tennis, playgrounds and concerts as well as colourful displays continue to delight the many visitors to Harrogate.

ABOVE: **THE KURSAAL, 1905.** Bystanders view the comings and goings at the Kursaal. Known today as the Royal Hall, it was opened in 1903 by Sir Hubert Parry, the composer of the music for *Jerusalem*. Many famous musicians have played at the hall including Sir Edward Elgar and Fritz Kreisler, as well as Joe Loss and the Beverley Sisters. The hall is still used today for performances, exhibitions and sporting events.

TWO VIEWS OF THE ROYAL PUMP ROOM: Centre, 1900 and left, 1905. The Pump Room was built in 1842 directly over one of Harrogate's sulphur wells to provide cover for the rich and famous who came to imbibe the waters. The waters can still be tasted but the Pump Room is now a museum chronicling the history of the spa.

SCARBOROUGH

For centuries Scarborough has attracted seaside visitors to its splendid bays and vies for the title of the oldest British seaside resort. Its history extends back much further to Norman times when the Earl of Holderness built the castle and redeveloped the town. The town received a royal charter from Henry II in 1166.

ABOVE: **BEACH ARCADE, 1913.** Ladies in linen outside "Arcadia" on the foreshore at Scarborough. The arcade was built to provide entertainments for the many visitors coming to Scarborough to try the often bracing sea waters. Plays, variety shows and sporting events such as boxing were all on offer. "Arcadia" has long since disappeared. Behind stands the Grand Hotel which opened in 1867 to international acclaim with 365 rooms, one for every day of the year.

RIGHT: **SCARBOROUGH SEAFRONT, 1913.** Edwardian bathers may have shown more decorum than those of modern times but they were no less enthusiastic about enjoying the delights of Scarborough. Along the esplanade the magnificent spa buildings can be seen. Today these are in use as a conference centre and theatre.

ABOVE: **THE FLORAL HALL, 1913.** Visitors promenade in front of the Floral Hall. It opened in 1911 and was one of Scarborough's many places of entertainment. People staying in guesthouses were encouraged to be out of the house as much as possible and this ensured a good audience for shows of all kinds. The Alexandra bowls centre is now on the site of the Floral Hall.

RIGHT: **SOUTH BAY POOL, 1930.** Crowds enjoy South Bay Pool which at 330ft (100m) long and 167ft (51m) wide was the largest outdoor pool in Europe. It was begun in 1914 and completed in 1915. Filled with seawater, the pool is a testament to the new social ideas of healthy urban living that gripped the early 20th century. Today it lies abandoned although the magnificent fountains are still intact.

ABOVE: **SCARBOROUGH BEACH, 1952.** Buckets and spades and paddling in the sea are perhaps the hallmarks of a day at a traditional British seaside resort. With two safe sandy beaches Scarborough was the perfect place for a family outing.

RIGHT: **FISH 'N' CHIPS, 1952.** Fish and chips is perhaps the national dish, and stalls such as this one are common even today, providing a relatively cheap and satisfying meal after a healthy day on the beach.

BELOW: **SIDESHOW, 1931.** The eager faces of children watching a Punch and Judy show in Scarborough. Punch and Judy can be seen as a very macabre story, gruesome even, dealing as it does with love and death, ghosts and ghouls, and murder and mayhem. But with its element of slapstick, and its sausage-eating crocodile, it has entertained young and old for generations.

FILEY AND BRIDLINGTON

If Scarborough represented the up-market end of seaside holidays, Filey and Bridlington always appealed to a more mass market audience. The advent of the railways brought holiday-makers to these fishing villages; by the mid 1950s visitors were flocking to both towns in tens of thousands.

Left: **YORKSHIRE BEACH, 1913.** Building sandcastles on the beach at Bridlington has been a popular pastime for generations. Behind the beach the splendid buildings of Royal Princes Parade and the sea defences can be seen. The parade was opened in 1888 and named in honour of Prince Albert.

Right: **THE HARBOUR AT BRIDLINGTON, *c*1930.** Boats and people throng the harbour at Bridlington. Fishing is still important to the life of the town, and catches are landed every day. Until the mid 19th century shipbuilding and the transport of grain were also part of life in Bridlington. But the advent of the railway was a mixed blessing, bringing tourists on the one hand but displacing the town's grain trade on the other.

Left: **PLOUGHING THE SANDS, 1937.** Bridlington bathers help to plough up the sands, in order to build up the beach against the bracing seas which are a feature of this coast.

Right: **FISHING COBLES, 1905.** Visitors being taken out by cart to fishing boats known as "cobles". These boats were designed to be launched off the gently sloping but often stormy beaches of the east and north-east coasts. In the 1880s there were 190 of these boats registered in Filey. Today there are preservation societies dedicated to keeping the coble in operation.

Bottom: **FILEY BEACH, 1921.** Bathing tents, such as those seen here at Filey, could be wheeled down the beach to the water's edge thus preserving the bathers' modesty.

ABOVE: **BUTLIN'S CANTEEN, 1946.**
Holidaymakers eating dinner
in the Butlin's canteen.
Butlin's at Filey was the third
of Billy Butlin's great mass
tourist centres. The year 1946
was its first fully in operation,
after use by the RAF during
the war. It had its own railway
station and at its peak in 1969
accommodated 10,000 visitors
at any one time. It was a
complete resort with
everything provided on site.
But as tastes changed so did
the viability of Butlins and the
camp closed in 1984.

WHITBY

Whitby and its near neighbour, Robin Hood's Bay, are two of the most historic places on Yorkshire's northern coastline. Whitby – home of explorer James Cook – is the site of an ancient abbey and has a colourful heritage of fishing and whaling. Today, the picturesque colour-washed stone cottages and cobbled streets of Robin Hood's Bay are a popular tourist haven – but the town has a long history of smuggling.

ABOVE: **SAILING SHIPS, 1900**. Sailing ships crowds Whitby's upper harbour. On the hill above the town lie the ruins of the 13th-century abbey, long used by seafarers to guide them up the Esk estuary to safe harbour in the town.

RIGHT: **WHITBY TOWN, 1931**. Townsfolk climb the 199 steps – known locally as Jacob's Ladder – linking the town with St Mary's Church sited close to the abbey on the east cliff overlooking the town. The steps contain resting places where pall-bearers stopped when carrying coffins up to the church for burial.

LEFT: **WHITBY BAY, 1913**. This panoramic shot looking across the river Esk shows the swing bridge built in 1909 linking the east and west sides of the town. The bridge divides the upper from the lower harbour and is built in two halves.

ABOVE: **WHITBY BEACH, 1924.** Looking along the west beach towards Sandsend. Since the development of the town as a seaside resort, Whitby built a county-wide reputation – still preserved to this day – for the quality of its fish and chips.

BELOW: **ARTIST'S PARADISE, 1910.** Two artists paint a deserted boat on the beach below Robin Hood's Bay. This calm scene belies the often ferocious storms which have taken their toll on the town. In 1780 high tides and raging seas caused a collapse in the limestone cliffs and 22 cottages tumbled into the sea.

ABOVE: **WHITBY SUNDAY MORNING, 1945.** Fishermen enjoy a gossip on the quayside. A house on the harbour front today houses a museum where the famous explorer James Cook lodged as an apprentice seaman. All of the ships Cook used on his famous voyages – Endeavour, Resolution, Adventure, and Discovery – were built in the town's local shipyard.

RIGHT: **WORKING OUTSIDE, 1935.** Women enjoy the sunshine while sitting outside a house in Robin Hood's Bay mending clothes. Until well into the 20th century the village remained remote, cut off by high cliffs and the narrow road which, to this day, remains almost impassable to traffic. Due to its isolation, smuggling was rife and it was said that "a bale of silk could pass from the bottom of the village to the top without seeing daylight" thanks to the connecting cellars running between the closely-packed houses.

THE YORKSHIRE DALES

The rugged uplands of the Yorkshire Dales have for centuries attracted visitors who come to enjoy its outstanding scenery, rich cultural heritage and charming towns and villages. There are over 20 main dales, each of which has its own special atmosphere.

RIGHT: **AYSGARTH FALLS, WENSLEYDALE, 1950.** The stunning Aysgarth Falls stretch for almost one mile along the River Ure through a wooded gorge. They are at their most spectacular after heavy rain.

ABOVE: **SETTLE MARKET, 1930.** Townsfolk chat and meet friends at the market. Settle is situated beneath the majestic limestone Castlebergh Rock. It has been a market town since the market charter was granted in 1249. The Market Square is still the hub of the town, surrounded by 17th-century buildings including the unusual two-storey arched Shambles, originally butchers and slaughterhouses.

RIGHT: **LEYBURN MARKET, 1930.** Farmers cluster around the agricultural goods for sale. Leyburn lies at the gateway to Wensleydale and has been a market town for hundreds of years with shops set around its three cobbled squares. The town has produce and livestock markets every week.

BELOW: **SOLAR ECLIPSE, GIGGLESWICK, 1927.** Crowds gathered on a hilltop near Giggleswick to view the solar eclipse. This was the first total eclipse of the sun since 1724 and Giggleswick was the perfect place to observe it. The Royal Astronomical Society mounted an expedition to photograph the corona from the grounds of the famous Giggleswick school. The next total eclipse would not occur until 1999.

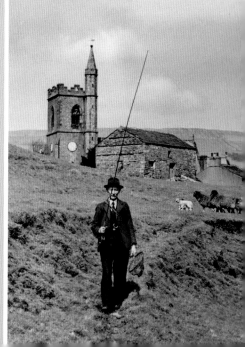

RIGHT: **UPPER WENSLEYDALE, 1950.** A lone fisherman walks past St Margaret's Church, Hawes on his way to the River Ure. St Margaret's was built in 1850 in the Gothic-style at a cost of £3,000. Hawes is the main town in Wensleydale and is famous for the production of Wensleydale cheese.

ABOVE AND BELOW: **TWO VIEWS OF KNARESBOROUGH**, *c*1900.
The river Nidd flows through a steep gorge in the market town of
Knaresborough, which lies on the edge of the Dales. The town's natural
beauty has attracted visitors for hundreds of years. In Victorian times
linen and cotton mills were established on the banks of the river; the
impressive railway viaduct was completed in 1854, linking the town to
York and Leeds. A spectacular water carnival was held every year, creating
a magical atmosphere as daylight faded. Today many tourists come to
explore the river either on foot or by boat.

ABOVE: **REPAIR JOB, 1936.** A
young woman takes time
to adjust her make-up by
the banks of the tranquil
River Nidd near to
Knaresborough. The river
flows from the wild fells
of Great Whernside to
the rich pastures of the
Vale of York.

ABOVE: **TWO VIEWS OF HAWORTH**, the Pennine village to the north of
Bradford where the Bronte family lived and where Emily, Charlotte and
Anne embarked on their literary careers. TOP: the village in 1955; BELOW:
Haworth Parsonage, *c*1860. In this house lived the most remarkable
literary family, all of whom had ambitions to write. It was here that they
constructed their imaginary world and later went on to produce works
such as *Wuthering Heights*, *Jane Eyre* and *The Tenant of Wildfell Hall*.
These great novels all resonate with the spirit of Yorkshire.

Published in 2011 by Myriad Books Limited
35 Bishopsthorpe Road, London SE26 4PA

Photographs copyright Getty Images
Text © copyright Susan Nowak

Susan Nowak has asserted her right under the Copyright, Designs and Patents Act,
1988, to be identified as the author of this work

ISBN 1 84746 257 X
EAN 978 1 84746 257 2

Designed by Jerry Goldie

Printed in China